HAL•LEONARD
INSTRUMENTAL
PLAY-ALONG

AUDIO
ACCESS
INCLUDED

PLAYBACK+
Speed • Pitch • Balance • Loop

CLARINET

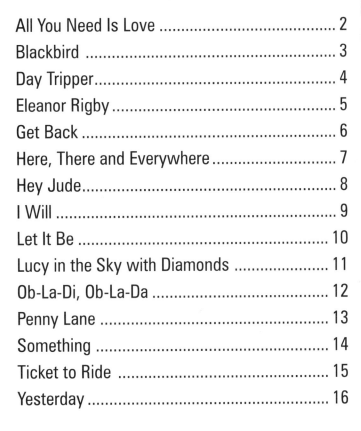

THE Beatles

T0081825

Cover Photo: Fiona Adams/Getty

To access audio visit:
www.halleonard.com/mylibrary

Enter Code
4031-6987-4572-3914

Audio Arrangements by Peter Deneff

ISBN 978-1-4950-9067-7

HAL•LEONARD®
7777 W. BLUEMOUND RD. P.O. BOX 13819 MILWAUKEE, WI 53213

In Australia Contact:
Hal Leonard Australia Pty. Ltd.
4 Lentara Court
Cheltenham, Victoria, 3192 Australia
Email: ausadmin@halleonard.com.au

Visit Hal Leonard Online at
www.halleonard.com

ALL YOU NEED IS LOVE

CLARINET

Words and Music by JOHN LENNON
and PAUL McCARTNEY

BLACKBIRD

Clarinet

Words and Music by JOHN LENNON
and PAUL McCARTNEY

DAY TRIPPER

CLARINET

Words and Music by JOHN LENNON
and PAUL McCARTNEY

ELEANOR RIGBY

Clarinet

Words and Music by JOHN LENNON
and PAUL McCARTNEY

GET BACK

CLARINET

Words and Music by JOHN LENNON
and PAUL McCARTNEY

HERE, THERE AND EVERYWHERE

Clarinet

Words and Music by JOHN LENNON
and PAUL McCARTNEY

HEY JUDE

CLARINET

Words and Music by JOHN LENNON
and PAUL McCARTNEY

I WILL

CLARINET

Words and Music by JOHN LENNON
and PAUL McCARTNEY

LET IT BE

CLARINET

Words and Music by JOHN LENNON
and PAUL McCARTNEY

LUCY IN THE SKY WITH DIAMONDS

CLARINET

Words and Music by JOHN LENNON
and PAUL McCARTNEY

OB-LA-DI, OB-LA-DA

CLARINET

Words and Music by JOHN LENNON
and PAUL McCARTNEY

PENNY LANE

CLARINET

Words and Music by JOHN LENNON
and PAUL McCARTNEY

SOMETHING

CLARINET

Words and Music by
GEORGE HARRISON

TICKET TO RIDE

CLARINET

Words and Music by JOHN LENNON
and PAUL McCARTNEY

YESTERDAY

CLARINET

Words and Music by JOHN LENNON
and PAUL McCARTNEY